An Anthology of Life

Poems by
Sirshendu Seal

©Sirshendu Seal 2021

All rights reserved
All rights reserved by author. No part of this publication may be reproduced, stored in a retrieval system or transmitted in any form or by any means, electronic, mechanical, photocopying, recording or otherwise, without the prior permission of the author.

Although every precaution has been taken to verify the accuracy of the information contained herein, the author and publisher assume no responsibility for any errors or omissions. No liability is assumed for damages that may result from the use of information contained within.

First Published in June 2021

ISBN: 978-93-5427-818-1

BLUEROSE PUBLISHERS
www.bluerosepublishers.com
info@bluerosepublishers.com
+91 8882 898 898

Cover Design:
Ananya Joshi

Typographic Design:
Vaishnavi Tiwari

Distributed by: BlueRose, Amazon, Flipkart

Dedicated to Sister Christine

(Principal, Holy Child School, Jalpaiguri)

Who in being the most virtuous person ever, is a constant inspiration to me.

About The Author

Sirshendu Seal is a student and a sprouting poet in his nineteens who writes poems about life and positivity in both English and Bengali.

He was born on 25th of August, 2001 at Alipurduar and was brought up in Jalpaiguri, W.B. while his roots being in Ghoksadanga, Cooch Behar. His parents are both well loved and revered school teachers.

From his childhood he has been a masterpiece student, excelling in sciences and languages. His academic achievements include being the topper in various National and International Olympiads. He is also a successful quizzer, an avid reader, circuit designer, and is also interested in recreational physics and recreational mathematics.

Apart from his academic excellence, he has in his pocket various awards in the fields of Western Dance, Photography, Essay Writing, Speech, Extempore, Western Singing and Painting. He has his own Rock Band named The Indian Masquerade.

He was living this life which might seem no less than a dream to many, then a sudden storm changed the route of his life and put him into ventilation. He faced two consecutive major brain surgeries within the span of a year. During this span, that is, after the first surgery, he was rendered paralyzed. It was due to his strong vital and mental power and, his mind over matter attitude that he has now returned to the normal phase of life. He has seen death very closely and returned from there. This journey to death and coming back has enriched his views on life. His present writings are a reflection of those.

Contacts:

Phone: +91 9547761952

E-Mail: sirshenduseal719@gmail.com

Instagram: @sirshenduseal

Facebook: Sirshendu Seal

Twitter: @SealSirshendu

FOREWORD

Sirshendu is a young, budding poet. His passion for penning down the thoughts of his young mind developed from his middle school days. He visualizes the world of the new generation from a distinct perspective. For him this cosmos is full of hope and possibilities. According to him, young minds should transcend beyond the limits of regular, mundane and pre-determined sets of goals. He says, one should try to explore the unexplored and experience the true essence of love and life.

His ideas make one realize that unlimited potentials exist in every human being.

I pray for his success and hope his lucid verses will help aspiring minds to realize the gossamer charms of this living world.

Mrs. Subrata Mitra
Senior English Teacher
Holy Child School,
Jalpaiguri,
West Bengal.

PREFACE

Positivity is the key to life. With optimism and determination we can achieve anything and everything. I have always been a believer of the "Everything is Possible" ideology.

In today's world, we are surrounded by negative thoughts and negativity. We can see anger, hatred and bigotry everywhere. Disturbed by this current state that the world is in, I thought of trying something new. After my keen observation, it had come to my notice that the young generation is in need of optimistic literary works. I felt this while I was in the ICU under ventilation. I could find very little of things that could help me inspire myself to live. I had attempted to start writing in the ICU itself but, after the brain surgery (which was performed under emergency conditions), I was rendered paralyzed and hence was not being able to write. But after I recovered from the peril, I knew what I was to do.

The following collection is an example of a few of my humble creations which depict life and its various aspects as I have seen them through my optimistic eyes.

The poems are for your own interpretation, they mean exactly what you think: there maybe literary devices, puns, double entendre, and everything else. It is all up to my respected and loved readers' wish how they want to interpret them.

Wish you all a happy reading.

Regards,
Sirshendu Seal

ACKNOWLEDGEMENTS

First of all I would like to thank all the readers for lending their precious time and energy towards my humble piece of work. I appreciate your patience and interpretation of the work.

I am grateful to the all loving God for blessing me with a third life.

I would love to mention my parents; without their love, care and support I would have never been the person I am today. Love you loads mom and dad.

I would like to thank all my teachers and the principal of my school, Sister Christine (Holy Child School, Jalpaiguri, West Bengal) who have always been very nice, caring and helpful. I especially thank all my English teachers throughout my school life under whose guidance I learnt the language. I express special gratitude towards my English teacher Subrata Ma'am (Mrs. Subrata Mitra, Senior English Teacher, Holy Child School, Jalpaiguri) for coming up with a wonderful well written Forewords' page.

I would like to thank Dr. Parag Kumar Agarwal, Dr. S R Sharma (North Bengal Neuro Centre, Pradhan Nagar, Siliguri, West Bengal) and, their colleagues and staff who have given me a new life after I had almost died due to AVM rupture and following complications. They literally revived me twice from ventilation.

I would like to acknowledge Pawel Sir (Mr. Pawel Khawas, Physiotherapist, North Bengal Neuro Centre) whose hard work and dedication has helped me recover from my paralysed state in which I was rendered after my first brain surgery.

Dr. Paritosh Pandey (Manipal Hospital, Bangalore) of whom I would forever be in debt as he has given me a new, healthy life. He was the one who performed a surgery and removed my second AVM.

I express my gratitude towards my friends, all the students and supporting staff of Holy Child School, for never leaving my side.

I would like to mention the various musical artists who have been a constant inspiration to life for me. They are the usual suspects: Ozzy Osbourne, Black Sabbath, The Doors, Bon Jovi, Led Zeppelin, Iron Maiden, The Beatles, Bob Dylan, David Bowie, Rabindranath Tagore (as a poet), Ravi Shankar, Mr. Big, Shakti, Mahavishnu Orchestra, Scorpions, Dio, Queen, Guns N Roses, Nirvana, Megadeth, Metallica, Whitesnake, A-Ha, Judas Priest, Steve Vai, Dragonforce, Moheener Ghoraguli, Artcell, The Who, Joe Satriani, Pink Floyd, Fleetwood Mac, Creedence Clearwater Revival, Aerosmith, The Eagles, Billy Joel, Bryan Adams, Pearl Jam, The Police, KISS, Audioslave, Soundgarden, Alice In Chains, Temple Of The Dog, Oasis, Green Day, Eminem and Yelawolf.

Last but not the least; I would like to thank my friends Siddhartha Banerjee, Gunjjan Pandey, Astha Roy and Shayeri Ray for helping me edit the work.

Yours Truly,

Sirshendu Seal

Contents

Mind over Matter 1

The Beautiful Journey of Life 2

Beautiful Life 3

The Man with a Thousand Faces 4

The Night's Hope 5

Yellow Dreams (Part I) 6

Yellow Dreams (Part II) 7

Yellow Dreams (Part III) 8

Dream Catcher 9

Man on the Moon 10

Sweet Relief 11

Strange Disease (Part I) 13

Strange Disease (Part II) 14

Strange Disease (Part III) 15

And I'm Waiting 16

Ode to the Maker 17

Ode to the Songbird 18

Strange Fallacies 19

Morning Light 20

An Eye for You 21

Sleepless Nights' Walk 22

Sunny Day's Rain 23

You Will Never Break My Heart 24

Stormy Night 25

Rolling Tears 26

Secret Chords 27

The Song of Life 28

I Am on My Way 29

Love Caught 30

Sleepless Nights 31

Grey Kaleidoscope 32

Sweet Summer 33

Autumn 34

Spring 35

The Summer Sun 36

The Rainy Day 37

Well Hidden 38

Drowsy Legs 39

Sleeptalks 40

Don't Wake Me Now 41

Lost My Way Back to There 42

Miracles 43

Fairy Lights 44

Kingdom of No Pain 45

True Perfection 46

Stranger 47

The Show 48

Tears 49

O Poet 50

Sea Shore 51

Rain Dance 52

Puddles 53

Snow 54

Comfort Zone 55

Morning Glory 56

Good Feelings 57

Blue Tin Box 58

December 59

The Park 60

Crowley's Song 61

Alternative Optimism 63

Like a Bird 64

The Night's Masquerade 66

The River 67

Lonely Heart 68

Call of the Wild 69

The Secret Garden of Bliss 70

Stranger and New Utopia 71

Starlight's Magic	72
Again on Promises	73
Love's Fallacy	74
The Magic Robe	75
Communication	76
Nature's Eyes	77
Camel Caravans	78
Phantoms	79
Atlantis	80
Riddle	81
Time Stops	83
Superhero	84
All The Way From The Start	85
Rock Music	87
War	88
Love	89
Meeting	90
The Painter	91
The Master of His Own	92
Road to Nowhere	93
Changes	94
Privileges	95
Rescue Me	96

Testament	97
The Song of Nature	99
The Master of my Life	100
Same Old Aching Heart	101
Same Old Feeling	102
The Songbird	103
The Singer	104
City of Glory	106
Starlight	107
On the Way of Life	108
The Perspective	109
Evolution (Still Animals)	110
Language	111
Dream	112
Rock 'N' Roll, The Savior	113
Learn To Forget	114
Time	115
True Wisdom	116
Chakra	117
Happiness	118
Sweet Youthful Beliefs	119
Perception	120
Hiraeth	121

Rise 122

Diary (Mind) 123

New Life 124

Paranoia 125

Society 126

The Love of God 127

New Day 128

Us and Us 129

Love Cage 130

Everlast 131

Mind over Matter

I know we all are down at times,

We stand at the verge of losing hope.

When we are cornered,

And we are pushed back.

But I say you, hold on,

Even if it needs your teeth and nails.

The brighter day is not so far,

The gloomy night is about to end.

I have always been a fighter too,

In the toughest of the times I never gave up.

It will be raining forever,

You must rise above the clouds;

For there is no use looking for a shelter,

Just let your will find you a way.

The Beautiful Journey of Life

I wonder how beautiful this life is!
This life of endless joy, filled with ecstasy,
The life is but a journey through,
The good times and the bad.

Oh it makes me wonder!
It really makes me wonder,
The wondrous journey of life;
The beautiful journey of life.

Come hold my hand-
Join me in the journey,
In the cozy voyage,
On the never ending streets of dream.

Beautiful Life

Sometimes across the screen of Facebook,
Sometimes beyond the world of Instagram-
Have you wondered, how beautiful-
Have you wondered how beautiful life is?

As you look through the blue screen-
Have you ever looked up to the sky?
Except for halogen and neon lights,
Have you ever looked up to the blue sky?

The starry night, soothing to the weary sight,
Does it amaze you too?
The constellations, the Man on the Moon-
All waiting to welcome you.

The Man with a Thousand Faces

Across the street I met someone,
But I could bet I saw none-
The man out of nowhere.

He said he was my friend,
And it hit me with a surprise for-
I never met him before!

He left in hurry-
Left with me a piece of paper,
Which said, "With Love,
From the Man with a Thousand Faces."

The Night's Hope

As the night falls strange in the city-
A strange weariness takes its grip on me.
It amazes me as it does you,
As we still have miles to go.

The night bird sings its evening notes,
The owls take their flight.
My heart is not empty but the empty roads-
They do make me sigh.

A strange drowsiness fills my head,
The streets all dead asleep.
The night is not forever,
The new day will dawn soon.

Yellow Dreams (Part I)

The yellow flowers and the sweet scent of summer-
    The sun and sunshine.
The starry sky and the yellow moon,
    Yellow flowers they come alive!

The moment that you wake from dreaming,
    You wake into a yellow dream.
Yellow dreams they give you signs and-
    You never know what they mean.

Yellow Dreams (Part II)

Yellow dreams pulled my heart away-
    Stole myself from me.
Yellow dreams took my heart away,
    Turned my life into a dream.

Yellow dreams do you show me today-
    What tomorrow will bring?
    Or you are just like another,
    Pleasant, cozy: daydream?

Yellow Dreams (Part III)

There comes the rain,

All my sunny days they drain.

No, I could not stop them-

What was to happen, did happen.

Everything I thought would stay-

Went away, went away rather too soon.

Nothing that was to happen could I presume,

What elapsed I could not resume.

No one came to stop the rain-

As would happen in a fairytale.

But my hopes still stick upon,

Upon my yellow dreams.

Dream Catcher

The signs on the wall,
Which show you all-
The quills with which,
Dreams are written.

The roads we used to stroll,
Which took us above it all-
Come in my dreams,
As every night closes in.

For I am in love with dreaming,
And I don't want to stay awake,
The master will come-
My soul to take.

Is there some spell cast on me?
Or am I day dreaming?
All my nightmares they have ceased,
Only good feelings, they exist.

Man on the Moon

O Man on the Moon,

With your pile of sticks;

And your dog,

How well are you?

There is someone out there,

I'm not really sure how he looks,

All our dreams he took,

He has stolen.

O Man on the Moon,

Did he fill your head-

All full of petty lies?

It seems to be that.

O Man on the Moon,

I am really grateful,

For returning my dreams,

To me.

Sweet Relief

Deep inside the eye of the mind,
Seeps in the glass, the sands of time-
Love in love lies,
Life does so too.

And as the sun begins to set,
The dusk begins to fall.
The birds seek for a dry place,
Somewhere they can call home.

People return from work-
Fields are all mown.
Love on the fields were grown,
Sights repain sighs.

Shadows slowly grow taller-
Taller than our souls.
For soul is all I am left with,
And I don't know what is right.

All I see turns to brown,
As the sun burns the ground;

And my eyes fill with sand,

As I scan the desert land.

Try to find your mind-

Try to find your heart-

Try to find your soul-

Try to find what you feel.

Strange Disease (Part I)

Everything is vogue and dizzy-
I need somewhere calm and cozy,
To lay down my head-
Some place where I would find serenity.

Forms in strange disguises-
Forms of strange disease,
Some call it heartbreak:
Some call it bliss.

In the temple of no discrimination,
You say we all are same.
O father of four winds-
Who will fill my sails?

I can sense you punish my wrongs,
Everywhere forfeits.
In life's fretted journey-
Which way is my life steering?

Strange Disease (Part II)

Strange days have come,
With the strange disease.
People seem stranger than ever,
Strange thoughts fill my head.

All my casual joys have been ripped,
All my senses have been stripped,
All my elation has been shred,
With the tears that have been shed.

Strange days have come,
With a strange disease;
In the temple of no God,
Everyone seems same to me.

Everybody is the hero,
I am the disease;
This is the way they make me feel,
This is the way they make me feel.

Strange Disease (Part III)

Fresh perfume fills the air,

As fresh music I hear.

Happiness is contagious-

I can see it dancing in the light.

In this world's strange business,

Happiness brings new light.

Life is happy, as long as you utilize-

Every second in good deeds,

For the strange disease,

This is the cure,

What more the world needs?

And I'm Waiting

Hey you sitting out there-

Can you hear me?

I'm cold.

My body feels no nothing, and I'm wondering

All my senses have gone numb,

From the toes to the thumb.

The weather it looks so fine,

I don't know why I'm left behind.

I am waiting for an Angel,

Who will come to rescue me.

I know someday she will come-

I know someday she will come,

And I'm waiting.

Ode to the Maker

I read these books of old,
I see nothing has been foretold-
I see nothing has been foretold,
I look for rays of hope.

I scan the empire of dusk,
On my magic sailing ship;
In this sea of dreams that is too deep,
And I am looking for you.

The story is not over yet-
Not at least for me.
I wonder what will happen next,
I wonder what the maker has in store for me.

Ode to the Songbird

Oh songbird-

You sing sweet songs,

You sing for the ones-

Who are right or wrong,

Would you sing a song for me?

Oh my little songbird-

You sing sweet songs for everyone,

You sing on the busy streets-

You sing on the lonely fields

Would you sing a song for me?

Oh dear little songbird-

You have such a sweet voice-

Among the world all full of noise,

Among the haze and turmoil:

Would you sing a song for me?

Strange Fallacies

Strange days filled with-
Strange fallacies.
The thief of dreams,
The thief of fantasies.

My brain is squirming like a toad-
As I am treading the empty roads.
The streets they seem unknown,
The fog is all I see.

If you take it for the truth-
You don't die- your soul forever flies,
Head all pierced with thorns-
The living, bear it all.

Morning Light

I am still waiting for the morning light,
For you said me you will take me away-
To that special place, where,
We used to see the morning light.

I guess I will be happy there-
I hope I will be happy then.
As I walk these empty roads,
Those cozy memories come into my head.

O the angel of my dreams,
Come let's go to that place-
Or maybe for a stroll in a park,
I want to see you again somehow.

Now as I walk alone in the land of no smiles,
Oh my mind full of thoughts,
All clustered into knots,
Won't you relieve them?

An Eye for You

Should I take control of my thoughts?
Before they bring me to rots:
Bring in things that I won't want.
How do I erase my head?

To the land of hopes you took me-
In the way you left.
Anywhere I see no one,
The lights they make me blind.

The happy days they are not over,
They are not I can say for sure.
For I still remember the days of elation,
In my head they will forever stay.

On the cozy bed of roses,
In the land of nobody-
With no one else to hold my hand;
I will have an eye for you:
An eye for you I will have.

Sleepless Nights' Walk

I keep walking through these nights,
Keep scanning the land;
Looking in the midnight sun,
Our memories made in moonlight.

My eyes they hate sleep,
For, the dreams they betray me.
The wise, they never let me speak-
The fools, they never believe me.

In the sleepless night's lost empire,
Will they ever prize your dreams?
In the world that has been lost,
To sprees of misbelieve and lack of trust.

I still stay awake and carry on my walk,
Journey of life carries on,
Looking at midnight fairies' dance,
I carry on with my sleepless night's walk.

Sunny Day's Rain

As the cloud beneath the sea-
So far away I fail to see,
Send the Rain-
All to me.

Maybe I just wanted to know-
Have you ever wondered,
How fun it would be?
If you could see the rain as I see,
Pouring down, on a sunny day.

You Will Never Break My Heart

I know the setting sun,

Can never shine again,

Inside, my beating heart still bleeding-

I never understood what you meant.

I heard time heals, hearts congeal;

My endless hours of wasted moments:

Our emotions juxtaposed,

Petty emotions all exaggerated.

Lonely hours I spend alone,

Filled with every moment-

Of stabbing daggers:

As I chafe my burnt hands beneath broken glass.

I try to find the shattered-

Pieces of my heart,

I know you will never break me again,

I know you will never break my heart.

Stormy Night

Through the stormy nights,
Exhausted horse's neighs-
To the riders on the storm,
The rain it gives in a silhouette.

My brain reeling thoughts of nothing,
My feet taking me home.
My mind runs fast as flash, feet lag behind;
Sweet memories never die.

In this longest night-
Of the year I must say;
The cold winds they chill my bones,
The wind howls, calls me home.

Rolling Tears

I am crying can you hear my sobs?
I am weeping can you see my tears?
The tears are rolling down.
My heart, it aches, hands go numb.

My drowsiness it amazes me-
I thought life had just begun,
Miles I thought I was to run;
Is it time for leaving already?

Though one thing I can be sure,
I will try until the very end,
For the sleeping they feel no pain-
Rolling tears know no bounds.

Secret Chords

The air feels so good-
The weather looks so fine,
The past is left behind;
Am I dreaming?

I look at the blue Sky,
I feel the warm sunshine,
I grab my guitar,
And play my secret chords.

They open me a gate,
Into the secret garden-
Of everlasting joy,
That never ends.

The Song of Life

I am wondering and wandering,

In this place that is so unknown;

I hear riffs I have never known,

Or did they hide from me?

I knew every note-

But I cannot remember now,

The secret chords that-

You shall never know.

Life is a song,

The songbird it sings:

I find it familiar-

It is all the same.

I Am on My Way

I am on my way,

Walking through nights-

Walking through days.

I am on my way,

To myself all the-

Brave stories I say.

I am on my way,

I am so excited-

No I cannot wait.

I am on my way-

I am on the way:

I cannot wait to be there.

Love Caught

On my way, on a bright Sunday-
I halted by a lake.
There I saw from a distance,
Someone coming by.

She stopped by me,
We exchanged "Hi"-
I felt something strange:
I did not fall in love;
I got caught by love.

Sleepless Nights

It is almost dawn,

I see the sun,

Rising above the horizon.

I try not to think,

About last night-

A sleepless night.

A sleepless night,

Without a blink,

With no sleep.

A night without sleep,

Among all others,

Just tears rolling down.

Grey Kaleidoscope

I got myself a kaleidoscope,
From a small shop on my way.
I thought it would show me-
Colours of the day.

But all I could see,
Were a million shades-
Some light some dark-
But all of grey.

Sweet Summer

I won't look back,

I won't look back now.

The miles I have walked,

The memories they stand true.

The sweet summer dreams,

The starry nights,

The graceful sights-

But I will never look back.

Maybe I will love you,

When the sweet summer-

Comes round the corner:

I will love you in summertime.

I will love you when,

The sweet summer comes in:

I will love you in the-

Sweet summer days.

Autumn

I love you and I do love you,
Maybe I will remember you-
Remember you oh through the,
Through the sweet autumn days.

O dreary autumn days-
Do you remember I met you,
I met you first in the autumn,
But before spring brought in
The blossoms, you walked away.

This time as the autumn comes in,
I will try to stay awake:
So you never come again-
My heart to break.

Spring

The spring comes in again,
Stimulating the nature;
Spring comes in again,
My favorite time of the year.

The spring I know her well,
I know her every moves.
With her magic wand,
She brings in life everywhere.

But spring I tell you,
She's a thief.
She stole from me,
My loneliness, my heart.

The Summer Sun

The summer sun,

As it seems to me-

Is not just Red and Orange,

It seems to me,

As if it were some-

Strange ball of colours.

A strange ball of colours-

With gold and silver hues.

It makes me wonder,

Perhaps makes me think:

How beautiful is life-

How beautiful life is.

The Rainy Day

After the sun, the rain comes in,

Just like they all said:

"It will rain a sunny day"

I did not believe them,

Now I am facing the consequences.

Good men say great things-

Fools their ears they plug.

Great things come to-

Those who wait;

But no one stops the rain.

I do not mind,

As I love walking in the rain.

I do not need no umbrella,

I love getting wet.

Good men they do good jobs-

And evil suffer in the end;

But all I pray for now is that:

Please don't stop the rain.

Well Hidden

As I wake up in the morning,

I see the morning sun-

With rays like mitotic threads.

The sun to it's rays,

As the birds to their wings-

And horses to their legs.

I wonder if there is,

Some supernatural conspiracy,

Well hidden behind the sun.

Drowsy Legs

The sun settles down,
It is just another day.

The legs, they are too tired to walk:
Too tired to step.

Little stars twinkling-
Twinkling above my head.

My eyes they show no drowsiness-
Much unlike my legs.

Sleeptalks

The night sky, like a blanket,
It covers the earth-
As I walk the roads,
With her on my side.

I tell her that I love her,
She says she loves me too.
A same old love story,
With nothing new.

The only difference is-
She is not with me,
I am on my own-
I wish she ever knew that,
I loved her like my own.

Don't Wake Me Now

I see a light in the wonderwall-
Or is it a crack in the sky?
Sleeping in darkness,
Or shall we call it night?

The Earth she rotates,
In the blink of an eye.
The night is over,
I see the light.

The skyline seems so blue-
Like a painter's easel.
The air I breathe it seems,
Fresh as the day.

Is this life or I am still dreaming?
For all that I see is all I ever wanted.
If this is a dream then,
Don't wake me up again.

Lost My Way Back to There

I wish I could go back,

To all those sunny days.

I wish I could have met before,

The ones that I'm learning about now.

I wish I could feel then,

As I am doing now-

I could hold my feelings back,

When I should have done.

I guess that my wish,

Will continue to be so:

For maybe I have lost my way,

Back to there.

Miracles

After the night is over,

A new day it comes.

Good things I try to-

Wonder about.

Sad things I try,

To forget on my way.

Wonderful world I have-

Been dreaming about.

Beautiful things come to-

Good men I see.

And the past it,

Buries its dead.

Miracles they happen,

Everywhere everywhile.

Good things keep happening,

If you do try.

Fairy Lights

Night sky,

The stars seem-

As if they were,

Fairy lights.

My dream-

They seem to seem,

My fancies

And fantasies.

All come alive-

When I am on my way,

The fairy lights they-

Show me the way.

The lights they-

Cannot blind me:

The sun will never-

Outshine me:

I am on my way.

Kingdom of No Pain

We all are kings and queens,
In this kingdom of happiness.
The kingdom of no sorrow,
The kingdom of endless bliss.

We are all blessed here,
No one is unblessed;
For we only know joy,
We know no pain.

This could be us,
Only if we tried,
The Earth could be as one-
Kingdom of Forever Joy.

True Perfection

The mountains are blue,

The fields they are green:

I love this life of elation-

Very much indeed.

Everything that is the creation:

Of us or the supreme-

Is truly perfect:

For, true perfection,

Has to be imperfect.

Stranger

On my way I see strangers-
Unknown faces all around.
It is nothing but eeriness,
I keep feeling all along.

I am just a stranger,
A new boy in the town-
Is there no one to befriend me?
To show me all around?

This could be my hometown-
I could show you,
All the by-lanes and by-ways;
But in this new town I am lost.

I see all the strangers,
No kin- no friends.
I hope I find someone,
Someone near and dear.

The Show

So the show,

The show they thought was over,

But I say not yet:

Not till I am breathing-

My final breath.

Nothing is yet over,

It is just the beginning:

So much more to do-

Roads yet to walk,

Life:

Life has just begun,

A new beginning;

End of all ends.

The life will forever go on.

Tears

What else can I afford-
To give you:
More than love?

What else can I afford-
To hold in my hands:
Than your hands?

What else can I afford-
To hold back from you:
Than my tears?

This could be a love song,
But it is drenched in tears-
How can love reside,
Where pain does?

O Poet

O poet what do you write?
Do you write about green fields-
About the blue sky.

O dear poet, the painter of dreams-
The believer of goodness-
The lover of words.

O dear poet-
Will you write for me?
Never shall I read then:
Anything other than thee.

Sea Shore

The moist smell of air that I breathe,
The blue horizon that I see;
The yellow sand I tread:
Never fail to amaze me.

The distant ship at the horizon,
The seagulls in the air.
The shops spread all around-
Make it a year round fair.

As the dusk begins to set in,
With its vivid show of colours-
The lighthouse sends out rays of light.
The crabs run helter-skelter.

Rain Dance

Here comes the rain again,

Old happiness they bring again,

I love the smell of rain;

I love dancing in the rain.

I tune into some Creedence Clearwater song,

As I warm myself up and dry up,

But one thing that I cannot deny-

I love dancing in the rain.

Puddles

Long as I remember,

Playing in the rain-

Childhood fantasies,

All getting wet.

Jumping into puddles,

Splashing mud all the way:

O good old childhood days,

Please don't go away.

Snow

Snowing, it's December,

Far away from home.

Hands gone numb;

But I love the thrill.

Snowballs and hot soup to sip,

I really love the feel.

Everything was so perfect:

I really want to go back there.

Oh I love snow:

Yes I love snow;

The snow so white and pure.

Comfort Zone

Cozy places may not always be the best,
For there might be a fire burning under.
This fire might be the end of everything;
Everything you ever loved.

Comfort zone is where dreams die,
Life is however a very easy business.
Life is very simple and easy,
But we strive to make it difficult.

Morning Glory

I woke up this morning-
The sun was shining down.
I went to the rooftop,
To watch the sun shine.

I look at the sunflowers,
The morning's beauty-
To meet the sun they are:
As eager as me.

I look at the flowers,
The morning glory.
The sweet smell that-
Comes off the flowers slowly.

Good Feelings

I hear the birds chirping:

Music of morning.

I call in my bandmates:

Morning's practice.

They bring me a new song-

Led Zeppelin maybe.

They tell me we will sing that,

They tell me we will do that.

It is more than just a feeling,

Something more than just a feeling;

It feels like I've been dreaming-

Feeling all the good things.

Blue Tin Box

Do you remember?
All the moments we spent together-
All the fun we had and all the memories:
I guess they'll never fade.

The seeds we dropped on the ground-
Now flowers are in bloom;
Just you are not there to see them.
How I wish I was not missing you.

All those letters and pretty gifts-
That to me you gave, I
Have kept with care.

December

I waited all through the year,

And now it is here: December.

The sweetest time of the year,

The time of everlasting joy is here.

December means endless joy,

December means no more tears,

Sad days are all gone-

Best days are here.

As I lie down on the sun-lit field,

As I lie down on the grass-green field,

Running my hand on the cold steel rail,

Walking down the aisle I keep wondering.

December is a wondrous time,

Bringing the sweet memories back;

Memories of the sweet old love,

Best feelings all lie here.

The Park

Lending an ear to the wind,
Walking by the park,
On a sunny day,
Where everything is fine-
Everybody is wide awake,
Children are having fun;
I love strolling in the park:
Lying on the grass.

The children running up and down,
Children having fun.
I love to see their smiling face,
As bright as the dawn.

As the day comes to an end: dusk sets in,
The keeper comes out of his shed,
He says, "Thank You for coming,
It is over for today."

Crowley's Song

Silent night, holy night, curious eyes,
Mr. Crowley's nocturnal rapport,
Everything is calm and quiet,
The air is filled with a serious mystery.

Everyone is at the feast,
Mr. Crowley is pure for sure;
With his lifestyle that is tragic,
With all he lived is just his magic.

Like an ancient archaeologist,
Bringing to us the sacred light,
You for sure were foreseen,
By some sacred bright eye.

Now as foretold ages ago,
I hear that holy maiden's call,
Beckoning things of the past,
To show the thrill of everything.

As I bid my farewell,
On my white horse I ride,

As you all already know,
These are all symbolic verse.

Alternative Optimism

If at the end of the day,

You cannot see the glass half full:

If it is half empty in your eyes,

You should know,

It is time to fill it for yourself.

Like a Bird

Come see me fly high,

Not to the clouds,

Beyond the sky,

Free from all restrictions,

Fly beyond the sky.

Sky is no more the limit,

Because here we have,

Freedom for all,

And everything here,

Is all for freedom.

Come see me fly,

Fly high enough:

It makes the mountain shy,

Because I am something-

More than a Freebird.

Here see me leap-

From one star to another,

Sup with the Sun and dine with Jupiter,

Here I am a citizen of the greater universe,

Something beyond your imagination:

Of a parallel.

Listening to the Cherubins,

In an ocean of emeralds green.

I live in a world you have never been,

And I have wings.

Come see me fly,

Sky is not that high,

Here I soar to the top,

Higher than a Freebird.

The Night's Masquerade

We march through the endless night,
The stars shine bright like cat's eyes.
Moon, the night's light;
Gleams like yellow sapphire.

Trees, as I walk through them,
Seem like a walking masque,
The cicadas play the fancy music:
The fireflies hold the torches.

The River

The sandy riverside,

Boats are passing by,

Standing against the wind,

The wind from northwest.

I follow the Teesta-

As it flows by the Jubilee Park,

Listening to the sound-

Of the flowing river.

The gurgling sound,

The sandy banks,

The cool breeze,

In my hair,

My river she shows-

Her sheen.

Never spread too thin,

Flowing love by gallons.

Lonely Heart

Just like all the promises,
And the lonely highways,
My head is still empty,
And my heart still feels the pain.

I'm just another heart-
In need of rescue,
Who is hanging on to-
Promises and dreams.

Yesterday is gone,
Tomorrow I know-
Will never come,
And so you won't.

With my light of hope,
I keep waiting,
And ask the Lord to give me-
Strength to carry on.

Call of the Wild

The trees, just like a canopy-
Over the ever-soaked ground.
Through the sounds of the forest,
The cicadas and the peacocks:
I hear the call of the wild.

The only friend with me now-
Is, the highway which runs through,
The heart of the forest,
The greenery amazes me-
The freshness that I feel,
The call of the wild I hear,
The wilderness' call.

The Secret Garden of Bliss

Hiding myself behind a door,
I found a key to my heart.
It took away my fears-
Opened up my soul.

The secret garden of joy,
The garden of never-ending bliss,
Filled with perfumed flowers,
Filled with bright green trees.

Is it paradise? Is time already?
For I think I've come to heaven.
If not heaven, where can it be?
Or maybe I have been dreaming.

Stranger and New Utopia

On my way I meet many strangers,
Faces those are all unknown.
Some give a smile, some grim visages,
Some look really eerie.

Stranger, o Stranger,
Am I lost in my way?
I am set on my way,
For a new Utopia-
Or am I already there?

Starlight's Magic

Here I sit under the night sky,
Gazing at the twinkling stars,
Staring at the constellations,
    Till they come out real.

The hunter holds his bow strong,
His black dog following him.
I see each of them come alive-
    Starlight's magic it seems.

Writing in the starlight is magic,
The words they all come out real,
All the magic happens in starlight-
When the moon shines and sky is clear.

Again on Promises

I set out again on my own,

Down the road-

To see the world-

I have never known.

Again bound by promises,

That I am supposed to keep;

The promises of today,

Yesterday and days before.

Now that I have understood,

And I have made up my mind,

So I am wasting no more time,

I set out again on promises.

Love's Fallacy

You never loved me,
Now I can say for sure;
It was just a fallacy of mine,
And youthful fantasy of yours.

Giving up on promises,
You gave love a bad name.
Hanging on to promises,
I quietly watched your game.

An angel's smile was your mask,
How was I to tell?
That promising me heaven,
You would put me through hell.

I was locked up in a passion's prison,
I could never break free.
Once bitten, a million times shy,
I assure you, this is our last goodbye.

The Magic Robe

The wizard walks by,
Wearing his Magic Robe;
Spreading magic through his wand.

The evil powers all disappear,
When the wizard walks by.

Turning all our tears to joy,
The wizard walks by.

The sun and moon all pay heed,
When wearing the Robe,
The wizard his spells, he spills.

Communication

Communication cannot sometimes be denied,

Specially when your soul wants to speak.

Communication is not an option it is the way,

It needs no language when your soul is awake.

Talk,

Talk it out,

Talk it out loud,

Keep talking.

Nature's Eyes

Nature always observes.

She says nothing,

She does not retaliate,

She loves it when,

You let her be her way.

If you want to listen to birds,

Don't buy cages, plant trees.

Nature sees you.

Camel Caravans

Camels, caravan they bear,
They see no oasis near,
Not a drop to drink,
Not a drop to quench thirst.

Endless sea of sand,
No water, everywhere land.
The trees of sweet dates-
Scar the desert land.

Seems like I am in some-
Scorching furnace of brick.
Bedouins their horses they race-
They move past us bid goodbye.

Phantoms

The phantoms and ghosts,
Cross my path endless times.

The phantoms and endless,
Ghosts of the night.

They call me from behind-
I close my eyes.

They come in front:
I close my eyes.

They make love to the night sky,
The phantoms of the night.

Atlantis

We are going far away,

Set for Atlantis,

Some thousand leagues-

Under the sea.

We are diving in the waters,

Plunging like the otters,

Going down and down below-

Under the blue waves.

In search of the treasures,

Beyond every measures,

We are more excited-

Than you ever were.

We are going deeper,

To reveal the secrets of Atlantis-

That you tried your very best to hide-

Hey Atlantis! Here we come.

Riddle

A matter that becomes clear-
Ceases to concern us,
So let there be ambiguity.

More complicated than-
The puzzle you are,
Clear as the daylight.

Useless in every sphere-
You are the:
Empty vessel that sounds much.

Empty mind with painful dreams,
Once bitten million times shy-
I try not to think of you.

Scribbling pages after pages,
It is better to sit back and relax,
Pure waste of the finite time

If staying back with you-
Meant being happy,

Then compared to that happiness,

    Million sorrows are better.

Time Stops

At times time stops-

And I stop dreaming.

Thinking of the promises,

And dreams of yesterday

Hanging on to the memories-

That I know I should better let go.

How I wish I were back there:

Living in the moment;

No worries about the day.

Time doesn't stop,

Neither does it come back, we know.

But for once let it be,

Not in reality, in my imagination let it be.

Superhero

I always had a dream,

Where the hero was a guy named me,

I could do pretty much anything.

There was no one to tell me what to do:

I was Free.

The girl I always dreamt of-

She was always with me.

Something more than your ordinary superhero,

I could do anything,

Not everything you told me to.

I had some special powers,

Could travel anywhere,

With anyone I cared.

Go round the world overnight,

With her holding me tight.

All The Way From The Start

Nothing ever gets me down-

You know this very well.

I am always fine,

And so shall I always be.

Nobody ever finds out,

The lies that hold up these lines.

Nobody ever does guess,

The pain I have been going through.

Do you even care if I wake up no more?

Do you even care if this journey ends-

And I get no chance to say goodbye?

Do you want to say goodbye?

Byes are never good,

Trust me as I say,

For going away-

Doesn't always mean forgetting.

I wish I could turn the time,

And change all the things-

Things that killed our love.

This can't be the end.

Rock Music

I was walking down a lonely dark road,
I was walking all alone, on my own.
I was feeling very dark and depressed,
I said to myself,"Lord, I need some space."
Then some hard music reached my ears,
Eased my mind, healed my wounds.
It soaked away all my tiredness-
I was feeling heavy, now no more.
Rock music saved my life,
So it did of many others.
Rock music heals all wounds-
Of mind-body-bosom-blood.
When will come the doomsday,
Heavy Metal will save the day.

War

I heard it in the air,

Closing in on the sphere.

Written in the air-

The rain-less clouds coming near.

Faces in the air,

Do you ever care?

Do we die as enemies?

Or live as brothers?

Coming in for days:

Mysterious ways.

Call of the duty,

For war or for peace.

Love

Love is in the air,

I can hear you everywhere.

How can it be so soon?

Why did you disappear?

I still remember,

The day I first met you,

A thrill filled winter morning;

Love was in the air.

Meeting

I hope in the future someday,

I will meet you again.

See you through the morning mist,

In the bright sunlight of the day.

I hope you would take me-

Take me back as I am.

For I can never change-

Never alter my ways.

The Painter

Vivid colours of beautiful life-

Million shaded rainbow,

The painter's palette reflects it all,

The colours are all well mixed up.

The tints, the hues,

The violets and blues,

The colours of joy and happiness-

The colours of morose and sorrow.

The colours with which-

He paints the world,

The colours they-

Shape our life:

The colours that impart happiness,

The colours that paint our joys.

The Master of His Own

Through the depths of the ocean,

The heights of the blue sky,

The master he moves on-

He swims, he flies.

Never to look behind,

He goes on walking-

The lonely roads again,

In the deserted town.

Desolate roads,

In the forbidden town,

Never to look back,

He moves on.

Road to Nowhere

Sometimes my feelings,
They just seem to-
Overpower me,
So helpless, I do feel.

The city's empty streets-
Are the only pathway,
I have ever known.
The starry sky is the-
Only roof above my head.

The city's neon signs-
Show me the way:
Come hit the road,
Along with me-
Road to nowhere,
Along with me.

Changes

You turned away,

To never return,

You faced away,

Eyes to never-

Meet again.

Still I keep waiting,

As I lie awake.

I know nothing,

Nothing can stay-

The same forever.

For change-

Is the nature of nature.

I guess my time has come,

To succumb to it and-

I am going through changes.

Privileges

Like a lifeless log I,

Hold on to the bank.

What I thought was an ocean,

Turned out to be a tank.

I see changing shapes of-

Nonexistent landscapes.

I dream of privileges-

That wise men seldom get.

Rescue Me

I can wait till the end,

Because I know,

It's not too late yet.

I am standing exactly where-

You left me.

My soul sides away,

As I reach out for you,

I've been waiting forever now,

Won't you come to rescue me?

Testament

Life will end in a death,
Death will never repay-
Only the good that you do,
Will make the next one's today.

Life is not for throwing away,
Neither for being unkind,
Love you spread will just stay-
Make next generation's today.

Life is really too short,
To slack and let it be,
There will come no tomorrow-
If you live in yesterdays.

Be strong,
Be brave,
Hold tight,
Through all that's done to you.

Try, you will know that you can,
Try, I know you can fly,

Don't get lost in the crowd,
You will for sure find a way.

Dreams are plans to be achieved,
Believe in them and you will succeed.
Tomorrow will never come,
Today will never end.

Be strong,
Hold tight,
In the storm,
Never let it go.

Truth will reign all over,
Love will be remembered,
No more taking the unimportant-
And leaving love behind.

The Song of Nature

Where the nature,

Is without fear;

Where the nature,

Sheds no tear;

Where the guns,

Kill no deer;

Where the flower,

Sprays its perfume;

Where the factories,

Spread no fume.

That is the place where,

Nature is free;

That is the place,

Where we can see,

The chuckle of-

The big tree;

The grin of the greenery,

And the blooming scenery.

The Master of my Life

I am the writer of my own story,

And one day the world will read it.

The master of my own ship-

The ruler of my own world.

The ring master of the circus-

The circus of my life.

To live life my own way,

Is the only way I believe.

Maybe you are the ace of spades,

But, I am the Joker of the deck.

Maybe you fly and soar high-

But I, I fly higher.

Same Old Aching Heart

I try to hum that old song,

We used to listen to-

For nights and days.

I have forgotten,

All the chords by now.

You try but can't sing that-

I try but can't play it out loud.

As I lie awake,

Under the open sky;

I feel that old pain-

The same old aching heart.

Same Old Feeling

The forgotten path which leads-
Into the sweet scented;
Garden of beautiful flowers-
Where the air plays music by itself.

Maybe this is the same feeling:
The same feeling I felt-
When I used to look towards the west;
With you right beside me.

I pray this not be another dream,
If it be so, I wish I never wake again.
And if I have to wake up;
I do so with you beside me.

The Songbird

The song of life it sings-
The beautiful little songbird,
It sings of rivers, sings of mountains:
Sings of streams, sings of trees.

Sing me a song, you are the songbird,
Sing me a song, o songbird-
My dear little Bird of Paradise,
Sing me a song, sing me a song.

This dull world makes me weary:
I am tired of its ways.
I wish it were not dead,
Void of emotions and thoughtless.

Sing me a song, you are the songbird-
The artist of my dreams.
My dear little Bird of Paradise,
Sing me a song, tonight-
O little songbird, sing me a song.

**The Singer**

The Singer he sings,

Songs of good days and bad.

Some soothing, some sad,

The Singer he sings.

The Singer he sings-

I guess the songs are for me;

For my life they do quote.

O Singer, are they all for me?

Some words are soothing,

Some are indeed polemic;

Some speak of life-

Some of death.

You have songs for everyone you say,

For lovers and losers,

For preachers and fools;

For all the people, even breakers of rules.

But I heard the songs,

Now I want to know what you meant.

Was it just fantasy,

Or polemically said?

City of Glory

My head is humming,
As I walk down the road;
Down the streets of dreams.

The whispering winds-
They tell the words of wisdom,
The distant verses of glory.

Down the streets of-
The city of glory,
I walk on my own.

The silent night,
When nobody's out;
I am on my own.

Starlight

I like writing in the starlight,

For it is when,

The words come out real.

I feel them, I see them,

I hear them and smell them-

All around me, all around.

The fact that I never grew up

Is because,

You cannot be a Rockstar,

And grow up at the same time.

You cannot lie awake-

And sleep in the same night.

On the Way of Life

On my way I have won and lost,

On my way I felt the heat and the frost,

On my way I have been through changes;

I've been weary and tired.

I have seen people growing love in their hearts,

Just like tunes- they come out of the lyre.

So far so good-

Love for all and all for love.

Just like made man's success,

And the Ace of Spade's gamble,

We can be sure as the Sun in the east;

Love will win.

All my life I've been learning-

Through the good times and bad,

Perseverance pays and-

Magic is for real.

The Perspective

People I meet and things I've seen,
Changed my perspective, the way I see.

The strange business of everyday life,
The rich they grow richer, the poor don't thrive.

I have seen things you say unreal,
I have met people who you say aren't there;
Come with me I will show you too.

The tune that opens up your soul-
I shall play for you.

The song we used to hum,
I shall sing for you.

Evolution (Still Animals)

I sit on the grass,

And see the animals grazing.

I know it is not a thing to gaze at,

You might as well think I am crazy.

I think about these animals:

I think about us;

I get a point to ponder-

It really makes me wonder.

We are all even being humans-

We all are still animals.

It reflects in the acts we do,

It takes wisdom to realize.

We are no different,

Than the others that walk the earth.

So I say unto you-

We aren't as much evolved as we think.

Language

We keep on talking all day,

Useless wastage of words,

Words they are offspring of language-

Language being the:

Manifestation of knowledge.

Knowledge is magical,

Magic is free;

It is everywhere-

If you have eyes to see.

Language 'PRETENDS' to communicate

The feelings you want to share,

Happiness and knowledge multiplies on sharing;

Sadness and sorrow decreases on doing so.

Dream

I am the dreamer,

And I know I'm not alone,

I am a dreamer,

And I dream of better days.

I am a dreamer,

And I know the world can change.

A blink of an eye is enough time,

For the world to be a better place.

So I ask everyone;

To dream on,

Dream till you fulfill your dreams,

Dream of better days and work on it,

Watch your dreams come true.

Dream on

Dream yourself a dream come true.

Rock 'N' Roll, The Savior

Rock and roll will save mankind,
Many a times I've said.
Open your heart, hear the guitar speak,
Heavy Metal, it is good for your brain.

Rock and Roll relieves all pain,
Heals all your scars and wounds,
Rock and Roll soothes your soul;
While keeping the fire inside you alive.

Save earth, because it is,
The only planet-
With Rock and Roll on it.
Rock and Roll will live forever,
If in it, you believe.

Learn To Forget

Learn to forget,

But never forget to learn.

Forget everything that is unpleasant,

Learn everything that is good.

At the end of the day,

It's only you that matters.

Time

Time passes by,

I keep walking on my way,

I am thinking straight,

My eyes on the road.

On my way I see many things,

I learn a lot never to forget.

I listen from wise men-

Also lend my ears to the fools.

One fine thing I can say,

Which will make your life like a sunny day;

Everything can wait but time will not-

Time will keep sliding away.

True Wisdom

Everything that is gold,

Need not always glitter.

Not all wandering people are lost.

The old and the aged-

Do not wither if strong.

Frost never reaches-

To the deepest of the roots.

The superficial roots,

Even if watered will come to rot.

Confined fish never knows,

The world outside the pot.

The water that flows,

Cannot be brought back.

True wisdom may come,

Before the grey hairs.

Magic that happens-

Cannot be denied.

Chakra

To live is the goal of life,
To die is the curse.
To live is the rarest in the world-
Most people just exist, that's all.

The visions of the oracle,
The prophet's prophecy-
All is vague if you don't believe;
Reel your head, make you feel dizzy.

The future never dies,
Life is a never ending wheel,
What you lose in this life,
You shall gather in another.

Happiness

You cannot buy happiness,

But you can be happy-

Even out of nothing.

For happiness is all within,

Within your heart and soul.

It is out of love that we are created;

For and out of love do we live,

Without love there is no meaning to life,

For all the rest is just misery-

And love breeds happiness within.

Sweet Youthful Beliefs

I have been all dreaming,

About sweet youthful beliefs-

That I have endless tomorrows.

I have been through it all;

Have seen the toughest around:

Now my body is my shrine.

Spreading the religion of-

Peace, love and music:

No hatred at all.

Come join me; we together,

Shall walk the earth.

Which would be a better place then.

The only thing that is holding you back-

Is your way of thinking.

Perception

Your eyes are your eyes,
Even if you cannot see through.
No one sees what you see;
Even if they see it too.

The world within your mind is
As beautiful as one outside.
Just a bit more colourful,
Joyful, lively and fanciful.

Life is a lesson, you keep learning
When you go through,
Through the doors of perception
Is how you do.

Diary (Mind)

I keep on writing in my diary,

The things I feel, I smell, I see.

I would really admit,

Mind is the best diary,

You never run out of pages,

No one breaches your privacy.

Verbal articulation is not the-

Way I express myself the best.

So I better write down a song or two,

Or may be even hum a tune.

The things they reel in my head;

Strange way I feel these days.

New Life

"It is all the same everyday"

You will never hear me say;

Every day is different in its way:

Nothing ever happens twice I say.

If you ever lived a life,

As exciting as I do;

I tell you - you will,

Never last a day.

I have seen my death,

Through my own eyes.

I defeated death with-

A firm, thunderous will,

And nothing I know is-

Going to be the same again.

Paranoia

I am concerned about my mental state!

Frowning in the morning,

Fully mad in the end.

Falling for the wrong things-

Letting go of the right.

I cannot take anymore-

Of this never ending fight.

I am so skeptical,

I doubt my own self.

After all these,

One thing scares me,

What if paranoia is real!

Society

Seeking and worshipping tyrants,

It is the age old practice of people.

People love to cooperate with and follow-

Restrictions and rules.

People love violence and are-

Enchanted by its majesty.

They despise freedom,

They despise liberty.

The Love of God

None that has taken birth,

Is inappropriate to be loved.

None that walks the earth,

Is too base to be loved.

None that walks the earth-

Is fit to be starved.

For we are the children,

Of the all loving God.

New Day

Someday we will live together-
With people who feel the same:
Feel with us the sun and the breeze.

Someday we will live as one-
In a world of no hatred,
And no scarcity.

One day will come as such,
We all will live peacefully.
And I firmly do believe-
The day is not far,
It will dawn soon.

Us and Us

Humans as we call ourselves,
Are we much better than the animals?
Or we are similar manifestations,
With false air of superiority?

You argue about difference between-
Us and the animals.
What I hear is difference between-
Us and Us.

We all are even being humans,
We are still animals.

Love Cage

Love is never forced,
What is forced cannot be love.

You don't force the one you love,
You never loved the one you force.

You never keep to yourself,
Everything you love-
You don't cage the beautiful-
Bird you adore the most.

Everlast

Nothing lasts forever,

Not even the bad days.

You cannot help it,

For change, it is,

The nature of nature.

Whatever you believe will last,

Is like everlasting belief

In ephemeral truths.

www.ingramcontent.com/pod-product-compliance
Ingram Content Group UK Ltd.
Pitfield, Milton Keynes, MK11 3LW, UK
UKHW022235230426
12048UKWH00018BA/1263